许渊冲经典
Version of Classical Chinese Poetry

宋词 下
Song Lyrics (II)

海豚出版社
中国国际出版集团

图书在版编目（CIP）数据

许渊冲经典英译古代诗歌1000首．宋词．下：汉英对照 / 许渊冲编译．-- 北京：海豚出版社，2012.9
ISBN 978-7-5110-1042-1

Ⅰ．①许… Ⅱ．①许… Ⅲ．①宋词－选集－汉、英 Ⅳ．①I222

中国版本图书馆CIP数据核字（2012）第202361号

总发行人：俞晓群

责任编辑：李忠孝　张　敏　王方志
责任印制：王瑞松
出　　版：海豚出版社有限责任公司
网　　址：http://www.dolphin-books.com.cn
地　　址：北京市西城区百万庄大街24号
邮　　编：100037
电　　话：010-68997480（销售）010-68998879（总编室）
传　　真：010-68998879
印　　刷：北京睿特印刷厂印刷
经　　销：全国新华书店
开　　本：32开（880毫米×1230毫米）
印　　张：3.5625
字　　数：28千
版　　次：2013年1月第1版　　2013年1月第1次印刷
标准书号：ISBN 978-7-5110-1042-1
定　　价：15.00元

版权所有　侵权必究

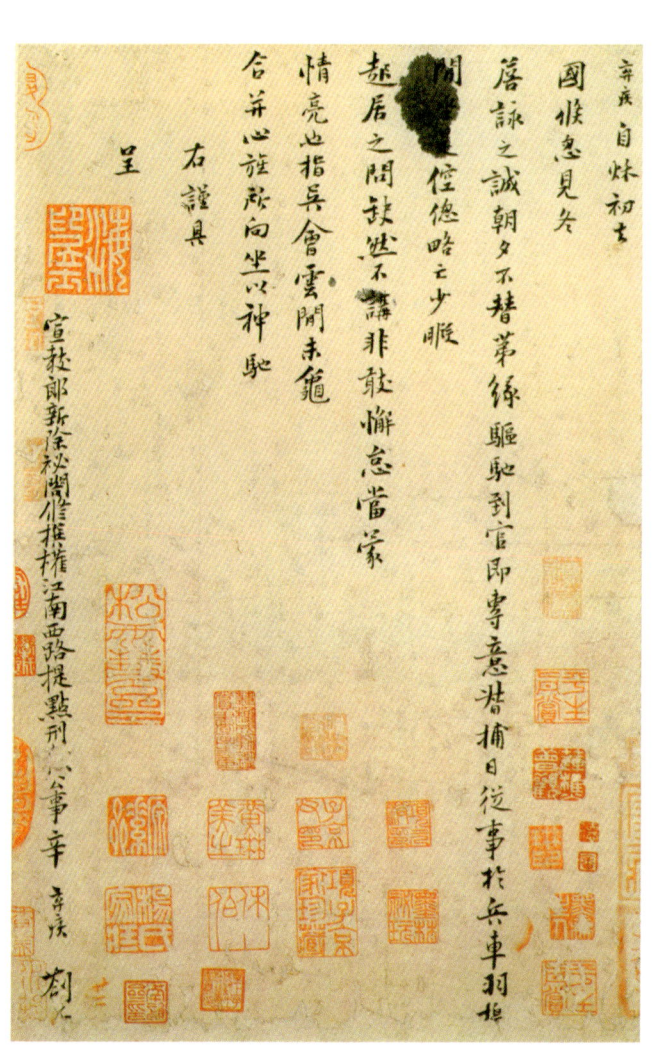

辛弃疾《去国帖》
Handwriting of Xin Qiji

煮茶画像砖（拓片）
Tea-brewing
(picture carved on brick)

梁楷《泼墨仙人图》
Picture of an Immortal
drawn by Liang Kai

杨无咎《墨梅图》
Picture of Mume Flowers
drawn by Yang Wujiu

陆游《自书诗卷》
Handwriting of Lu You

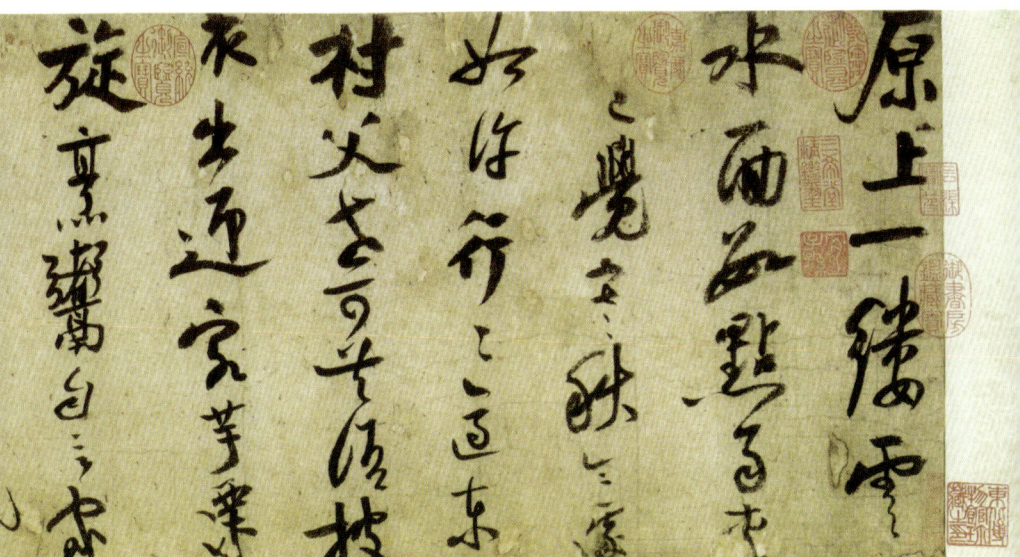

刘松年《撵茶图》
Tea Brewing
picture drawn by Liu Songnian

佚名《飞阁延风图》
Picture of a Sight-seeing Pavilion

许译中国古典诗词集序

2011年,我国提出了建设社会主义文化强国的号召。2012年,海豚出版社编印了十本许译中国古典诗词集,这就响应了在世界上建立文化强国的号召。其实,早在二千五百年前,中国已经是世界上的文化强国。那时西方有希腊、罗马文化,有苏格拉底、柏拉图的哲学,有荷马的史诗,东方却有中国文化,有孔子和老子的哲学,有《诗经》的风雅颂。西方的史诗歌颂英雄,歌颂战争,东方的《诗经》却歌颂人民,歌颂劳动。荷马史诗中歌颂英雄和战争的名句如:

冲锋陷阵我带头,论功行赏不落后。

《诗经·大雅》中的《公刘》却歌颂了公元前1796年周民族大迁移的民主劳动生活,如:

京师之野,(京师田野形势好,)

于时处处,(于是定居建新邦,)

于时庐旅,(于是规划造住房,)

于时言言,(谈笑风生喜洋洋,)

于时语语。(七嘴八舌闹嚷嚷。)(程俊英译)

建造住房是劳动生活,七嘴八舌是民主讨论。可见我国早在四千年前,已经有自由民主的劳动生活,并有《诗经》记录在案,比西方早了两千多年,因此,把我国的文化经典《诗经》、《唐诗》、《宋词》、《元曲》等译成外文,向全世界宣扬先进的中国古典文化,是把我国建设成为文化强国的重要部分,也是建设更加光辉灿烂的世界文化不可缺少的篇章。

现在世界上有十三亿人用中文,又有大约八亿人用英文,中文和英文是世界上用得最多,也是最重要的语文。因此,要在全世界宣扬中国文化,使中国成为文化强国,首先要把中文译成英文。如何进行翻译呢?现在西方用得最多的是美国奈达教授提出的"对等翻译"。但是奈达不懂中文,只能进行西方语文之间的翻译。而据电子计算机统计,西方语文(如英、法、德、俄、意、西)的词汇约有百分之九十可以在另一种西方语文中找到对等的表达方式,所以翻译时基本可以用对等原则。但是中文和西文不同,中文词汇大约只有百分之五十可以在西方语文中找到对等的表达方式。这就是说,中西互译时只有一半可以找到对等语,另一半却找不到。怎么办呢?那有两种可能:一种是译语的表达方式不如源语,那时只好不得已而求其次;另一种是译语优于源语,或超越了源语,那时,就应该尽可能发挥译语的优势,也就是用最好的译语表达方式,甚至超越源语,这就不是对等原则,而是超越原则了。下面就来举例说明。

唐代杜牧写了一首《清明》:"清明时节雨纷纷,路上行人欲断魂。借问酒家何处有?牧童遥指杏花村。"这首诗应该如何译成英文?能不能应用对等原则呢?首先,我们要问"清明"是不是天清气明,"时节"是不是时候或节日的意思?如果是,那"天清气明"的时节怎么又"雨纷纷"了?这不是矛盾吗?所以这里"清明"不是指天气,而是指悼念亡人的节日,译成英文,就不能选择字面上的对等语,而要选字面上不对等,却能传达原文意义的表达方式。其次,"纷纷"这个叠词在英文中也没有对等语。

一个英译本说是雨下得大,这种译文不如原文。另一种译文说:雨水像眼泪一般流下。这就超越原文了。但是考虑到原诗的主题是悼念亡人,把雨水比做眼泪更能体现哀悼之情,那译文就可以说是符合超越的原则了。第二句诗"路上行人"不是指一般的过路人,而是特指上坟悼念死者的亲友,所以译成英文不能用"行人"的对等词,而要用超越一般行人的"哀悼者"。下半句的"断魂"也没有英文的对等语,译成伤心可能略轻,译成心碎可能略重。一般认为过犹不及,我却认为"过之"可能胜于"不及"。第三句"借问"是婉转的说法,现代就会用"请问"了,英文可以不译,那却是以"不译"为"译"。"酒家"译成英文也是"形"对等而"实"不对等,因为英国的酒家太热闹,英文的"酒家"又可能指卖酒而不喝酒的酒店,所以严格说来并不对等。第四句的"牧童"有人译成"牛仔",那就"形"同而"实"不同了。"杏花村"是酒店的名字,真译成"村"也是有名无实,又是"形"对等而"实"不对等。所以四句诗内,多半都不对等,对等的只有第一句的"雨"字,第二句的"路上",第三句的"何处有",第四句的"遥指"二字。有对等词的诗句,翻译时可以用对等词,没有对等词时,应该根据什么原则来翻译呢?

《老子》第一章说:"道可道,非常道;名可名,非常名。"第一个"道"是名词,是"道理"的意思。第二个"道"是动词,是"说道"或"知道"的意思,那就是说,道理是可以知道的,但不一定是你所知道的道理;事物是可以有个名字的,但是名字并不等于实物。或者简单点说,"名"并不等于"实"。这个"道",包括翻译之道在内。所以翻译之道是可以知道的,但不一定是大家常说的"对等翻译"之道。至于"名可名"更可有几种解释:

一种是名称并不等于实物,应用到翻译上来,可以说原文并不等于原文所描写的现实;更进一步,又可以说,译文并不等于原文;再进一步,译文虽不一定等于原文,但距离原文所描写的现实,却不一定比原文更远。这就是老子关于翻译认识论的三步曲。联系到《清明》这首诗的翻译上来,"清明时节"并不等于"天清气明",这就是"名可名,非常名";而悼亡日却是"清明时节"所描写的现实,英译文用了"悼亡日",那就比原文距离现实更近了一步。这就是应用《老子》来发展中国文学翻译理论的例子。

至于孔子呢,《论语》第二章中说到"从心所欲不逾矩",朱光潜认为这是"一切艺术的成熟境界",自然也是翻译艺术的成熟境界。"从心所欲"就是要发挥译者的主观能动性,"不逾矩"就是不能超越规律。《清明》的英译文中,把"雨纷纷"说成"雨水与泪水齐飞",把借酒浇愁说成饮酒淹没哀思,都是"从心所欲不逾矩"的例子。这说明中国文学翻译已经进入"从心所欲"的自由王国,而西方翻译理论还在"不逾矩"的必然王国挣扎。由此可见,中国文学翻译的理论比西方更先进,那种认为中国译论落后于西方二十年的谬论,是没有根据的,是奴化思想的残余。至于实践,全世界只有中国人(包括华裔)出版了大量的中英互译作品,外国人没有一个出版过大量的中文文学作品的。因此,无论是理论或实践,中国翻译都走在世界前列,是建设世界文化强国的先声。

许渊冲 2012 年 8 月 18 日于北京大学

Preface

As early as three thousand years ago, China was a leading country in the world. So far as philosophy is concerned, there were Confucius and the Old Master in the 5th. century B. C. while in the West there were Socrates, Plato and Aristotle in the 4th B. C. So far as literature is concerned, we had our *Book of Poetry* while the West had Homer's epics *Iliad* and *Odyssey*. The difference is that Homer's epics glorify war and heroes while the *Book of Poetry* sings the praise of peace and the common people. For instance, in Homer's *Iliad* we find the wellknown couplet in *Hector's farewell address to Andromache*:

Where heroes war, the foremost place I claim,
The first in danger as the first in fame.

But in the Book of Poetry we find the following verse in *Duke Liu*, the second legendary hero of *the House of Zhou*, who moved from Tai to Bin in 1796 B. C. :

He built a new capital
For his people all.
Some thought it good for the throng,
Others would not dwell there for long.
There was discussion free:
They talked in high glee.

To build a new capital was hard labor, and discussion free showed that there was democracy in the throng. This verse glorifies the laboring life of the common people and their free discussion on the building of the capital. This shows that China enjoyed freedom and democracy far earlier than the West. Therefore, the translation of the *Book of Poetry* of Zhou dynasty, and poetry of other dyansties, such as *Tang poetry, Song lyrics,* and *Yuan songs,* will make Chinese culture known to the world on the one hand, and on the other, help the world make greater progress in political, economical and cultural development.

In the world of today, there are 1.3 billion people who use the Chinese language and about 800 million who use the English, so Chinese and English are the most important languages in the world, and the translation between them is also as important. But how to translate one into the other? In the West, Eugene Nida's translation theory is in vogue, that is the principle of dynamic equivalence. But Nida could only translate between Western languages and he did not understand the Chinese. Could his theory be applied to the translation between Chinese and English? According to statistics, about 90% of the vocabulary of one Western language can find its equivalent in another Western language. But between the Chinese and the English vocabulary, we can find no more than 50% of equivalence. That is to say, In translation between these two languages, the principle of equivalence can be applied only to half of the vocabulary of either language. Then how about the other half to which the principle cannot be applied? When there is equivalence between two words or expressions, one says as much as the other. When there is not, one says more or less, better or worse than the other. In this case, I prefer more to less, and better to worse. That is to say, if the target language cannot say as much as the source language, I think it better to say more than to say less than the original, to excel the original than to fail to express the original idea. Therefore, the theory I put forward may be called Principle of Excellence, that is, when the principle of equivalence cannot be applied, we may try to find a better or an excellent expression. This may be illustrated by examples. Following are two versions of the same poem, one follows the principle of equivalence and the other that of excellence.

(A) *It drizzles thick on the Pure Brightness Day;*
I travel with my heart lost in dismay.
"Is there a public house somewhere, cowboy?"
He points at Apricot Bloom Village faraway.

(B) *A drizzling rain falls like tears on the Mourning Day;*
The mourner's heart is going to break on his way.
Where can a wineshop be found to drown his sad hours?
A cowherd points to a cot 'mid apricot flowers.

The Pure Brightness Day is equivalent to the original in word but not in sense, for it is contradictory to say *it drizzles on a pure bright day*. On the contrary, *the Mourning Day* is not equivalent in word but succeeds in expressing the idea. *A drizzling rain falls like tears says* more than the oringinal while *it drizzles thick* says less.

Here I prefer more to less for the comparison between rain and tears makes the reader understand *the mourner's heart* in the second line. Likewise, *to drown his sad hours* also says more, but it also helps to understand why the mourner needs a wineshop. These examples show how to apply the principle of Excellence when that of Equivalence fails. As to further explication, please read the preface in Chinese.

Xu Yuanchong
Aug. 18, 2012, at Peking University

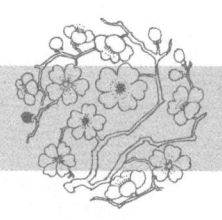 # 目 录

临江仙（晏几道） 3
蝶恋花（晏几道） 4
蝶恋花（晏几道） 6
生查子（晏几道） 8
清平乐（晏几道） 9
木兰花（晏几道） 11
玉楼春（晏几道） 12
鹧鸪天（晏几道） 14
生查子（晏几道） 15
浣溪沙（晏几道） 17
诉衷情（晏几道） 18
生查子（晏几道） 20

鹧鸪天（晏几道）……………………22

点绛唇（晏几道）……………………23

减字木兰花（王安国）………………25

清平乐（王安国）……………………26

菩萨蛮（王安石）……………………28

浣溪沙（王安石）……………………29

南乡子（王安石）……………………31

桂枝香（王安石）……………………32

青玉案（欧阳修）……………………35

蝶恋花（欧阳修）……………………37

蝶恋花（欧阳修）……………………39

诉衷情（欧阳修）……………………41

浪淘沙（欧阳修）……………………43

临江仙（欧阳修）……………………45

长相思（欧阳修）……………………47

望江南（欧阳修）……………………48

采桑子（欧阳修）……………………50

生查子（欧阳修）……………………52

西江月（司马光）……………………53

玉楼春（宋祁）………………………55

锦缠道（宋祁）……56
踏莎行（晏殊）……58
踏莎行（晏殊）……60
踏莎行（晏殊）……62
踏莎行（晏殊）……63
清平乐（晏殊）……65
清平乐（晏殊）……67
蝶恋花（晏殊）……68
蝶恋花（晏殊）……70
浣溪沙（晏殊）……72
浣溪沙（晏殊）……73
山亭柳（晏殊）……74
玉楼春（晏殊）……77
浣溪沙（晏殊）……78
离亭燕（张昇）……80
千秋岁（张先）……82
诉衷情（张先）……84
一丛花（张先）……86
菩萨蛮（张先）……88
天仙子（张先）……89

CONTENTS

Tune: Immortal at the River (*Yan Jidao*) 4

Tune: Butterflies over Flowers (*Yan Jidao*) 5

Tune: Butterflies over Flowers (*Yan Jidao*) 7

Tune: Mountain Hawthorn (*Yan Jidao*) 9

Tune: Pure, Serene Music (*Yan Jidao*) 10

Tune: Magnolia Flower (*Yan Jidao*) 12

Tune: Spring in Jade Pavilion (*Yan Jidao*) 13

Tune: Partridge Sky (*Yan Jidao*) 15

Tune: Mountain Hawthorn (*Yan Jidao*) 16

Tune: Silk-Washing Stream (*Yan Jidao*) 18

Tune: Telling of Innermost Feeling (*Yan Jidao*) 19

Tune: Mountain Hawthorn (*Yan Jidao*) 21

Tune: Partridge Sky (*Yan Jidao*) 22

Tune: Rouged Lips (*Yan Jidao*) 24

Tune: Shortened Form of Lily
    Magnolia Flowers (*Wang Anguo*) 26

Tune: Pure, Serene Music (*Wang Anguo*) 27

Tune: Buddhist Dancers (*Wang Anshi*) 29

Tune: Silk-Washing Stream (*Wang Anshi*) 30

Tune: A Southern Song (*Wang Anshi*) 32

Tune: Fragrance of Laurel Branch
    (*Wang Anshi*) 34

Tune: Green Jade Cup (*Ouyang Xiu*) 36

Tune: Butterflies over Flowers (*Ouyang Xiu*) 38

Tune: Butterflies over Flowers (*Ouyang Xiu*) 40

Tune: Telling of Innermost Feeling
    (*Ouyang Xiu*) 42

Tune: Ripples Sifting Sand (*Ouyang Xiu*) 44

Tune: Immortal at the River (*Ouyang Xiu*) 46

Tune: Everlasting Longing (*Ouyang Xiu*) 47

Tune: Dreaming of the South (*Ouyang Xiu*) 49

Tune: Song of Picking Mulberries
  (*Ouyang Xiu*) 51
Tune: Mountain Hawthorn (*Ouyang Xiu*) 52
Tune: The Moon over the West River
  (*Sima Guang*) 54
Tune: Spring in Jade Pavilion (*Song Qi*) 55
Tune: The Way of Brocade (*Song Qi*) 57
Tune: Treading on Grass (*Yan Shu*) 59
Tune: Treading on Grass (*Yan Shu*) 61
Tune: Treading on Grass (*Yan Shu*) 63
Tune: Treading on Grass (*Yan Shu*) 64
Tune: Pure, Serene Music (*Yan Shu*) 66
Tune: Pure, Serene Music (*Yan Shu*) 68
Tune: Butterflies over Flowers (*Yan Shu*) 69
Tune: Butterflies over Flowers (*Yan Shu*) 71
Tune: Silk-Washing Stream (*Yan Shu*) 72
Tune: Silk-Washing Stream (*Yan Shu*) 74
Tune: Willow by Mountainside Pavilion
  (*Yan Shu*) 76
Tune: Spring in Jade Pavilion (*Yan Shu*) 78

Tune: Silk-Washing Stream (*Yan Shu*) 79
Tune: Swallows Leaving Pavilion
  (*Zhang Bian*) 81
Tune: A Thousand Autumns (*Zhang Xian*) 83
Tune: Telling of Innermost Feeling
  (*Zhang Xian*) 85
Tune: Song of Flower Shrub (*Zhang Xian*) 87
Tune: Buddhist Dancers (*Zhang Xian*) 89
Tune: Song of the Immortal (*Zhang Xian*) 90

宋词 下
Song lyrics

临江仙

晏几道

梦后楼台高锁,
酒醒帘幕低垂。
去年春恨却来时。
落花人独立,
微雨燕双飞。

记得小蘋初见,
两重心字罗衣。
琵琶弦上说相思。
当时明月在,
曾照彩云归。

Tune: Immortal at the River

Yan Jidao

Awake from dreams, I find the locked tower high;
Sobered from wine, I see the curtain hanging low.
As last year spring grief seems to grow;
Amid the falling blooms alone stand I;
In the fine rain a pair of swallows fly.

I still remember when I first saw pretty Ping,
In silken dress embroidered with two hearts in a ring,
Revealing lovesickness by touching pipa's string.
The moon shines bright just as last year;
It did see her like a cloud disappear.

蝶恋花

晏几道

醉别西楼醒不记。

春梦秋云，
聚散真容易。
斜月半窗还少睡，
画屏闲展吴山翠。

衣上酒痕诗里字。
点点行行，
总是凄凉意。
红烛自怜无好计，
夜寒空替人垂泪。

Tune: Butterflies over Flowers

Yan Jidao

I don't remember my drunk hour
When we parted at Western Bower.
It's easy to part as to meet
Like autumn clouds or spring dreams sweet.

Into my window peep moonbeams, I cannot sleep;
The Southern Mountains green spread on the painted screen.

On my robe stains of wine
Just as words in my song,
Drop after drop, line after line.
Tell how my dreariness lasts long.
The candle pities its own helpless plight
And weeps in vain for me in the cold night.

蝶恋花

晏几道

梦入江南烟水路，
行尽江南，
不与离人遇。
睡里消魂无说处，
觉来惆怅消魂误。

yù jìn cǐ qíng shū chǐ sù
欲尽此情书尺素,
fú yàn chén yú
浮雁沉鱼,
zhōng liǎo wú píng jù
终了无凭据。
què yǐ huǎn xián gē bié xù
却倚缓弦歌别绪,
duàn cháng yí pò qín zhēng zhù
断肠移破秦筝柱。

Tune: Butterflies over Flowers

Yan Jidao

I dreamed of roving on the southern rivershore,
However far I might go,
I could not find the fair one I adore.
To whom could I tell of my woe?
Awake, I am as sorrow-laden as before.

I would put down my lovesickness in black and white,
No swan above nor fish below
Would bring to her the love letter I write.
I can but pluck the strings to sing my woe;

My broken heart would break the strings of zither tight.

生查子 (shēng zhā zǐ)

晏几道 (yàn jǐ dào)

关山魂梦长，
塞雁音尘少。
两鬓可怜青，
只为相思老。

归梦碧纱窗，
说与人人道：
"真个别离难，
不似相逢好。"

Tune: Mountain Hawthorn

Yan Jidao

Severed by far-off mountain pass,
The wild geese bring me letters few.
My temple hair once black, alas!
Turns grey only for missing you.

In dream I stood by window green
And told you whom I longed to meet:
"The grief of parting is so keen;
The joy of meeting is so sweet!"

qīng píng yuè
清 平 乐

yàn jǐ dào
晏 几 道

liú rén bú zhù
留 人 不 住 ,

zuì jiě lán zhōu qù
醉 解 兰 舟 去 。
yí zhào bì tāo chūn shuǐ lù
一 棹 碧 涛 春 水 路 ,
guò jìn xiǎo yīng tí chù
过 尽 晓 莺 啼 处 。

dù tóu yáng liǔ qīng qīng
渡 头 杨 柳 青 青 ,
zhī zhī yè yè lí qíng
枝 枝 叶 叶 离 情 。
cǐ hòu jǐn shū xiū jì
此 后 锦 书 休 寄 ,
huà lóu yún yǔ wú píng
画 楼 云 雨 无 凭 。

Tune: Pure, Serene Music

Yan Jidao

I could not persuade you to stay;
Drunk, you untied the cabled boat and went away.
Dipping the oars into green waves of spring,
You'd pass all trees where golden orioles sing.

The ferry's green with willows, leaf on leaf

And twig on twig reveal the parting grief.
Write no more letter if you forget the fresh shower
Brought by the cloud for thirsting flower!

木兰花 (mù lán huā)

晏几道 (yàn jǐ dào)

秋千院落重帘暮，
彩笔闲来题绣户。
墙头丹杏雨余花，
门外绿杨风后絮。

朝云信断知何处？
应作襄王春梦去。
紫骝认得旧游踪，
嘶过画桥东畔路。

Tune: Magnolia Flower

Yan Jidao

The sun sets over the garden swing and curtained bower;
Within embroidered doors my pen's made verse with ease.
Red apricots fade over the wall after the shower;
Green willow catkins out of doors waft in the breeze.

Where is my morning cloud leaving nor word nor trace?
She must have gone into another's vernal dream.
My piebald horse still knows my old-time roving place;
It neighs on passing painted bridge over eastern stream.

yù lóu chūn
玉楼春

yàn jǐ dào
晏几道

dōng fēng yòu zuò wú qíng jì
东 风 又 作 无 情 计 ,

yàn fěn jiāo hóng chuī mǎn dì
艳 粉 娇 红 吹 满 地 。
bì lóu lián yǐng bù zhē chóu
碧 楼 帘 影 不 遮 愁 ,
hái sì qù nián jīn rì yì
还 似 去 年 今 日 意 。

shuí zhī cuò guǎn chūn cán shì
谁 知 错 管 春 残 事 ,
dào chù dēng lín céng fèi lèi
到 处 登 临 曾 费 泪 。
cǐ shí jīn zhǎn zhí xū shēn
此 时 金 盏 直 须 深 ,
kàn jìn luò huā néng jǐ zuì
看 尽 落 花 能 几 醉 !

Tune: Spring in Jade Pavilion

Yan Jidao

The eastern wind has plotted the cruelest thing,
Blowing down petals red and rosy here and there.
The bower's curtain green can't hide my grief over spring.
Just as this day last year fall lovely blossoms fair.

Why should I by mistake over waning season weep?

How many tears have I shedded in lofty towers?
Now in the golden cup of wine I should drink deep.
How many times can I get drunk over fallen flowers!

鹧鸪天

晏几道

醉拍春衫惜旧香，
天将离恨恼疏狂。
年年陌上生秋草，
日日楼中到夕阳。

云渺渺，
水茫茫，
征人归路许多长。
相思本是无凭语，
莫向花笺费泪行！

Tune: Partridge Sky

Yan Jidao

Drunk, I caress my sleeves where perfume old won't pass.
Does mine remind them of caress of my dear one?
Each year of autumn's approach tells yellowing grass;
Each day the same message is brought by the setting sun.

Cloud on cloud drifting past
Melts into water vast.
How long the homeward way for wanderers appears!
"Longing" is honey-sweet, but it cannot long last.
Oh, write to her, but let no word be wet with tears!

shēng zhā zǐ
生 查 子

yàn jǐ dào
晏几道

zhuì yǔ yǐ cí yún
坠 雨 已 辞 云 ,

流水难归浦。
遗恨几时休?
心抵秋莲苦。

忍泪不能歌,
试托哀弦语。
弦语愿相逢,
知有相逢否?

Tune: Mountain Hawthorn

Yan Jidao

From clouds has fallen rain;
It can't go back again.
O when will end its grief to part?
Bitter as lotus seed's my heart.

Holding back my tears, I can't sing,

Confiding grief to my lute's string.
My heartstring wishes to meet you.
But, oh! could I meet you anew?

浣溪沙 huàn xī shā

晏几道 yàn jǐ dào

日日双眉斗画长,
rì rì shuāng méi dòu huà cháng

行云飞絮共轻狂。
xíng yún fēi xù gòng qīng kuáng

不将心嫁冶游郎。
bù jiāng xīn jià yě yóu láng

溅酒滴残歌扇字,
jiàn jiǔ dī cán gē shàn zì

弄花熏得舞衣香。
nòng huā xūn dé wǔ yī xiāng

一春弹泪说凄凉。
yì chūn tán lèi shuō qī liáng

Tune: Silk-Washing Stream

Yan Jidao

From day to day we vie in painting eyebrows long,
As light-hearted as wafting clouds and willow-down.
My heart won't wed a gallant fond of wine and song.

The wine I spilt left stains on my fan of songstress;
The flowers I played with perfumed my dancing gown.
Shedding tears all the spring, I tell my loneliness.

sù zhōng qíng
诉衷情

yàn jǐ dào
晏几道

cháng yīn huì cǎo jì luó qún
长因蕙草记罗裙,
lù yāo chén shuǐ xūn
绿腰沉水熏。

阑干曲处人静，
曾共倚黄昏。

风有韵，
月无痕，
暗销魂。
拟将幽恨，
试写残花，
寄与朝云。

Tune: Telling of Innermost Feeling

Yan Jidao

I oft remember your robe when green grass is seen,
Perfumed by incense burnt your girdle green.
Au is quiet along the balustrade,
On which we leaned when daylight began to fade.

The breeze is full of grace,
The moon has left no trace,
My soul is steeped in hidden grief.
And I would try
To write it on a withered flower or leaf
And send it to the morning cloud on high.

生查子 shēng zhā zǐ

晏几道 yàn jǐ dào

长恨涉江遥，
cháng hèn shè jiāng yáo

移近溪头住。
yí jìn xī tóu zhù

闲荡木兰舟，
xián dàng mù lán zhōu

误入双鸳浦。
wù rù shuāng yuān pǔ

无端轻薄云，
wú duān qīng bó yún

暗作帘纤雨。
àn zuò lián xiān yǔ

cuì xiù bù shēng hán
翠 袖 不 胜 寒 ,
yù xiàng hé huā yǔ
欲 向 荷 花 语 。

Tune: Mountain Hawthorn

Yan Jidao

She never likes to cross the river far
And moves toward its head, where lovebirds are.
She sets her orchid boat adrift at leisure
And goes astray like lovebirds seeking pleasure.

An unexpected fickle cloud unseen
Turns into drizzling rain behind the screen.
Her greenish sleeves can't stand the cold. To whom
Could she complain but to the lotus bloom?

鹧鸪天

晏几道

彩袖殷勤捧玉钟，
当年拚却醉颜红。
舞低杨柳楼心月，
歌尽桃花扇影风。

从别后，
忆相逢，
几回魂梦与君同！
今宵剩把银釭照，
犹恐相逢是梦中。

Tune: Partridge Sky

Yan Jidao

Time and again with rainbow sleeves you tried to fill

My cup with wine that, drunk, I kept on drinking still.
You danced and danced till the moon hung low over willow trees;
You sang and sang till amid peach blossoms blushed the breeze.

Then came the time to part,
But you're deep in my heart.
How many times have I met you in dreams at night!
Now left to gaze at you in silver candlelight,
I fear it is not you
But a sweet dream untrue.

diǎn jiàng chún
点绛唇

yàn jǐ dào
晏几道

huā xìn lái shí
花 信 来 时 ,
hèn wú rén sì huā yī jiù
恨 无 人 似 花 依 旧 。
yòu chéng chūn shòu
又 成 春 瘦 ,
zhé duàn mén qián liǔ
折 断 门 前 柳 。

tiān　yǔ　duō　qíng
天　与　多　情　,
bù　yǔ　zhǎng xiāng shǒu
不　与　长　相　守　。
fēn　fēi　hòu
分　飞　后　,
lèi　hén　huò　jiǔ
泪　痕　和　酒　,
zhān　le　shuāng luó　xiù
占　了　双　罗　袖　。

Tune: Rouged Lips

Yan Jidao

When flowers herald spring again,
Why won't my lord come back with flowers as before?
Now spring begins to wane;
I've broken all his willow twigs before the door.

Heaven above tells us to love.
Why are we kept apart so long?
Since he sang farewell song,
Even wine grieves,
Mingled with tears, it's stained my sleeves.

减字木兰花

王安国

画桥流水,
雨湿落红飞不起。
月破黄昏,
帘里余香马上闻。

徘徊不语,
今夜梦魂何处去?
不似垂杨,
犹解飞花入洞房。

Tune: Shortened Form of Lily Magnolia Flowers

Wang Anguo

Beneath painted bridge water flows by;
The fallen flowers wet with rain can no more fly.
The moon breaks through twilight;
Fragrance within the curtain's smelt ere I alight.

Silently lingering around,
Where will my dreaming soul tonight be found?
Unlike the weeping willow,
Whose down will fly into your room and on your pillow.

qīng píng yuè
清平乐

wáng ān guó
王安国

liú chūn bú zhù
留春不住，

费尽莺儿语。
满地残红宫锦污,
昨夜南园风雨。

小怜初上琵琶,
晓来思绕天涯。
不肯画堂朱户,
春风自在杨花。

Tune: Pure, Serene Music

Wang Anguo

Spring cannot be retained,
Though orioles have exhausted their song.
The ground is strewn with fallen reds like brocade stained,
The southern garden washed by rain all the night long.

For the first time the songstress plucked pipa string;
At dawn her yearning soars into the sky.

The painted hall with crimson door's no place for spring;
The vernal breeze with willow down wafts high.

菩萨蛮
集句
王安石

海棠乱发皆临水,
君知此处花何似?
凉月白纷纷,
香风隔岸闻。

啭枝黄鸟近,
隔岸声相应。
随意坐莓苔,
飘零酒一杯。

Tune: Buddhist Dancers
Old Verses Rearranged

Wang Anshi

By waterside the crabapple flowers run riot;
You know what they look like on rivershore so quiet.
In cold moonlight while petals fall with ease,
Across the stream blows fragrant breeze.

Golden orioles warble on the tree nearby;
Their warbling echoes low and high.
I sit as I please on moss fine,
Stroll or float with a cup of wine.

huàn xī shā
浣溪沙

wáng ān shí
王安石

bǎi mǔ zhōng tíng bàn shì tái
百亩中庭半是苔，

門前白道水縈回。
愛閒能有幾人來？

小院回廊春寂寂，
山桃溪杏兩三栽。
為誰零落為誰開？

Tune: Silk-Washing Stream

Wang Anshi

Half moss-hidden is my courtyard a hundred acres wide,
Before my gate a winding path by riverside.
Who would visit one fond of leisure and free hours?

Spring in my courtyard girt with corridors is still;
Two or three peach and apricot trees stand near the hill.
For whom are they blooming and then fall in showers?

南乡子

王安石

自古帝王州,
郁郁葱葱佳气浮。
四百年来成一梦,
堪愁。
晋代衣冠成古丘。

绕水恣行游,
上尽层城更上楼。
往事悠悠君莫问,
回头。
槛外长江空自流。

Tune: A Southern Song

Wang Anshi

The capital was ruled by kings since days gone by.
The rich green and lush gloom breathe a majestic sigh.
Like dreams has passed the reign of four hundred long years,
Which calls forth tears.
Ancient laureates are buried like their ancient peers.

Along the river I go where I will;
Up city walls and watch towers I gaze my fill.
Do not ask what has passed without leaving a trail!
To what avail?
The endless river rolls in vain beyond the rail.

---

guì zhī xiāng
桂枝香

wáng ān shí
王安石

dēng lín sòng mù
登临送目，

zhèng gù guó wǎn qiū
正故国晚秋，
tiān qì chū sù
天气初肃。
qiān lǐ chéng jiāng sì liàn
千里澄江似练，
cuì fēng rú cù
翠峰如簇。
zhēng fān qù zhào cán yáng lǐ
征帆去棹残阳里，
bèi xī fēng jiǔ qí xié chù
背西风酒旗斜矗。
cǎi zhōu yún dàn
彩舟云淡，
xīng hé lù qǐ
星河鹭起，
huà tú nán zú
画图难足。

niàn wǎng xī fán huá jìng zhú
念往昔繁华竞逐，
tàn mén wài lóu tóu
叹门外楼头，
bēi hèn xiāng xù
悲恨相续。
qiān gǔ píng gāo duì cǐ
千古凭高对此，
màn jiē róng rǔ
漫嗟荣辱。
liù cháo jiù shì suí liú shuǐ
六朝旧事随流水，
dàn hán yān shuāi cǎo níng lù
但寒烟衰草凝绿。
zhì jīn shāng nǚ
至今商女，

shí shí yóu chàng,
时 时 犹 唱 ,
　　　　　hòu tíng　　yí　qǔ
《 后 庭 》 遗 曲 。

Tune: Fragrance of Laurel Branch

Wang Anshi

I climb a height

And strain my sight;

Of autumn late it is the coldest time;

The ancient capital looks sublime.

The limpid river, beltlike, flows a thousand miles;

Emerald peak on peak towers in piles.

In the declining sun sails come and go;

In the west wind wineshop flags flutter high and low.

The painted boat

In clouds afloat,

Like stars in Silver River egrets fly.

What a picture before the eye!

The days gone by
Saw people in opulence vie.
Alas! Shame came on shame under the walls,
In palace halls.
Leaning on rails, in vain I utter sighs
Over ancient kingdoms' fall and rise.
The running water saw the Six Dynasties pass,
But I see only chilly mist and withered grass.
Even now the songstresses still sing
The songs composed by a captive king.

青玉案

欧阳修

一年春事都来几?
早过了
三之二。
绿暗红嫣浑可事。

绿杨庭院、
暖风帘幕,
有个人憔悴。
买花载酒长安市,
又争似
家山见桃李?
不枉东风吹客泪,
相思难表、
梦魂无据,
唯有归来是。

Tune: Green Jade Cup

Ouyang Xiu

How many happy things in the spring of a year?
Two-thirds of them have passed away.

Shady green leaves and red flowers appear
Cheerful and gay.
The courtyard shaded by willow trees
And curtains ruffed by warm breeze.
Alone I'm languid, ill at ease.

In the capital I buy flowers and drink wine.
How can they vie with peach and plum in homeland mine?
Why should the eastern breeze blow down my tears in streams?
It is hard to express my homesickness.
And I cannot rely on dreams.
To go home is the best of all the ways
To spend the rest of my days.

dié liàn huā
蝶恋花

ōu yáng xiū
欧阳修

tíng yuàn shēn shēn shēn jǐ xǔ
庭 院 深 深 深 几 许 ？
yáng liǔ duī yān
杨 柳 堆 烟 ，

lián mù wú chóng shù
帘幕无重数。
yù lè diāo ān yóu yě chù
玉勒雕鞍游冶处,
lóu gāo bú jiàn zhāng tái lù
楼高不见章台路。

yǔ héng fēng kuáng sān yuè mù
雨横风狂三月暮,
mén yǎn huáng hūn
门掩黄昏,
wú jì liú chūn zhù
无计留春住。
lèi yǎn wèn huā huā bù yǔ
泪眼问花花不语,
luàn hóng fēi guò qiū qiān qù
乱红飞过秋千去。

Tune: Butterflies over Flowers

Ouyang Xiu

Deep, deep the courtyard where he is, so deep.

It's veiled by smokelike willows heap on heap.

By curtain on curtain and screen on screen.

Leaving his saddle and bridle, there he has been

Merry-making. from my tower his trace can't be seen.

The third moon now, the wind and rain are raging late;
At dusk I bar the gate,
But I can't bar in spring.
My tearful eyes ask flowers, but they fail to bring
An answer. I see red blooms fly over the swing.

蝶恋花 (dié liàn huā)

欧阳修 (ōu yáng xiū)

几日行云何处去？
jǐ rì xíng yún hé chù qù

忘了归来，
wàng le guī lái

不道春将暮。
bú dào chūn jiāng mù

百草千花寒食路，
bǎi cǎo qiān huā hán shí lù

香车系在谁家树？
xiāng chē jì zài shuí jiā shù

泪眼倚楼频独语，
lèi yǎn yǐ lóu pín dú yǔ

双燕来时，
shuāng yàn lái shí

mò shàng xiāng féng fǒu？
　　陌　上　相　逢　否　？
　　liáo luàn chūn chóu rú liǔ xù
　　撩　乱　春　愁　如　柳　絮　，
　　yī yī mèng lǐ wú xún chù
　　依　依　梦　里　无　寻　处　。

Tune: Butterflies over Flowers

Ouyang Xiu

Where have you gone like cloud from day to day
Forgetting to come homeward way?
Don't you know spring has grown old and late?
Flowers and grass by roadside teem on Cold Food Day.
Under whose tree is your scented cab and at whose gate?

Alone on balcony, with tearful eyes I query
A pair of returning swallows, dreary,
Whether they have met you on the pathway?
Spring grief is running wild like willowdown, it seems;
Nowhere can I find you, even in my lonely dreams.

诉衷情

欧阳修

清晨帘幕卷轻霜,
呵手试梅妆。
都缘自有离恨,
故画作远山长。

思往事,
惜流光,
易成伤。
未歌先敛,
欲笑还颦,
最断人肠。

Tune: Telling of Innermost Feeling

Ouyang Xiu

At dawn she rolls up window screen
And a light frost is seen.
She breathes to warm her hands so fair
And adorns with mume blossoms her hair.
As she nurses the parting sorrow still,
She pencils her brows like a distant hill.

As she recalls the past,
She regrets time flies fast;
Her heart would ache.
Before she sings, she pauses awhile;
She knits her brows when she would smile.
Oh, whose heart would not break!

浪淘沙

欧阳修

把酒祝东风,
且共从容。
垂杨紫陌洛城东。
总是旧时携手处,
游遍芳丛。

聚散苦匆匆,
此恨无穷。
今年花胜去年红。
可惜明年花更好,
知与谁同?

Tune: Ripples Sifting Sand

Ouyang Xiu

Wine cup in hand, I drink to eastern breeze:
Let us empty with ease!
On the violet pathways
Green with willows east of the capital,
We used to stroll hand in hand in bygone days,
Rambling past flower shrubs one and all.

To meet in haste and part
Would ever break the heart.
Flowers this year redder than last appear.
Next year more beautiful they'll be.
But who will enjoy them with me?

临江仙

欧阳修

柳外轻雷池上雨,
雨声滴碎荷声。
小楼西角断虹明。
阑干私倚处,
遥见月华生。

燕子飞来窥画栋,
玉钩垂下帘旌。
凉波不动簟纹平。
水晶双枕畔,
犹有堕钗横。

Tune: Immortal at the River

Ouyang Xiu

The thunder faints away beyond the willows green;
The raindrops drip from lotus leaves after the shower.
An imperfect rainbow is seen,
Shut out of view by Western Tower.
We lean on rails alone
To watch the rising moon.

A pair of swallows flies back to the painted eave;
Through fallen curtain they peep and perceive
The wavy mat still spread
Cold on the bed
As if none had slept in,
But by the crystal pillows twin
There is left a hairpin.

长相思

欧阳修

萍满溪，
柳绕堤，
相送行人溪水西。
回时陇月低。

烟霏霏，
雨凄凄，
重倚朱门听马嘶。
寒鸥相对飞。

Tune: Everlasting Longing

Ouyang Xiu

A creek full of duckweed,

Winding with green willow trees,

On western shore I bade my parting friend goodbye.

When I came back, the moon hung low over the hill.

On mist-veiled rill

Blows chilly breeze.

Leaning on painted gate

Again I wait

For my friend's neighing steed;

I see gulls fly

Pair by pair

In cold air.

wàng jiāng nán
望 江 南

ōu yáng xiū
欧阳修

jiāng nán liǔ
江 南 柳 ,
huā liǔ liǎng xiāng róu
花 柳 两 相 柔 。

花片落叶黏酒盏，
柳条低处拂人头，
各自是风流。

江南月，
如镜复如钩。
似镜不侵红粉面，
似钩不挂画帘头，
长是照离愁。

Tune: Dreaming of the South

Ouyang Xiu

See Southern willow trees
To slender flowers smile with ease!
The fallen petals will adorn your cup of wine;
The willow branches hanging low caress your head,
Each inch a beauty spread.

See the Southern moon look
Now like a mirror, now like a hook:
A mirror in which no rosy faces shine;
A hook on which hangs no curtain red;
It ever shines on sleeple bed.

cǎi sāng zǐ
采桑子

ōu yáng xiū
欧阳修

huà chuán zài jiǔ xī hú hǎo
画 船 载 酒 西 湖 好,
jí guǎn fán xián
急 管 繁 弦,
yù zhǎn cuī chuán
玉 盏 催 传,
wěn fàn píng bō rèn zuì mián
稳 泛 平 波 任 醉 眠。

xíng yún què zài xíng zhōu xià
行 云 却 在 行 舟 下,
kōng shuǐ chéng xiān
空 水 澄 鲜,
fǔ yǎng liú lián
俯 仰 留 连,

yí shì hú zhōng bié yǒu tiān
疑是湖中别有天。

Tune: Song of Picking Mulberries

Ouyang Xiu

West Lake is fine for us in painted boat loaded with wine.
From pipes and strings comes music fast;
From hand to hand jade cup soon passed.
Secure on calming waves and drunk we lie.

Fleeting clouds seem to float beneath our moving boat.
The sky seems near to water clear.
Looking up and below; away we will not go.
It seems there's in there's lake another sky.

生查子

欧阳修

含羞整翠鬟，
得意频相顾。
雁柱十三弦，
一一春莺语。

娇云容易飞，
梦断知何处？
深院锁黄昏，
阵阵芭蕉雨。

Tune: Mountain Hawthorn

Ouyang Xiu

Shy, she arranges her hair adorned with jade,

And often looks at me when a tune is well played.
Like rows of wild geese slant her thirteen strings;
As oriole's vernal song note on note sings.

Easy to fly away the fair cloud seems.
Where can l find her, awake from my dreams?
Locked up with the twilight in my bower.
I hear on banana leaves fall shower on shower.

xī jiāng yuè
西江月

sī mǎ guāng
司马光

bǎo jì sōng sōng wǎn jiù
宝髻松松挽就,
qiān huá dàn dàn zhuāng chéng
铅华淡淡妆成。
hóng yān cuì wù zhào qīng yíng
红烟翠雾罩轻盈,
fēi xù yóu sī wú dìng
飞絮游丝无定。

xiāng jiàn zěn rú bú jiàn
相见争如不见,

yǒu qíng huán sì wú qíng
有 情 还 似 无 情 。
shēng gē sàn hòu jiǔ wēi xǐng
笙 歌 散 后 酒 微 醒 ,
shēn yuàn yuè míng rén jìng
深 院 月 明 人 静 。

Tune: The Moon over the West River

Sima Guang

Loosely she has done up her hair;
Thinly she has powdered her face.
In rosy smoke and purple mist she looks so fair;
As light as willowdown she walks with grace.

Before we part, we long to meet;
Amorous, she seems not in love.
Awake from wine and songs so sweet.
The courtyard is still and bright the moon above.

玉楼春

宋祁

东城渐觉风光好,
縠绉波纹迎客棹。
绿杨烟外晓寒轻,
红杏枝头春意闹。

浮生长恨欢娱少,
肯爱千金轻一笑?
为君持酒劝斜阳,
且向花间留晚照。

Tune: Spring in Jade Pavilion

Song Qi

The scenery is getting fine east of the town;

The rippling water greets boats rowing up and down.
Beyond green willows morning chill is growing mild;
On pink apricot branches spring is running wild.

In our floating life scarce are pleasures we seek after.
How can we value gold above a hearty laughter?
I raise winecup to ask the slanting sun to stay
And leave among the flowers its departing ray.

jǐn chán dào
锦缠道

sòng qí
宋 祁

yàn zǐ ní nán
燕 子 呢 喃，
jǐng sè zhà cháng chūn zhòu
景 色 乍 长 春 昼。
dǔ yuán lín
睹 园 林、
wàn huā rú xiù
万 花 如 绣。
hǎi táng jīng yǔ yān zhī tòu
海 棠 经 雨 胭 脂 透。
liǔ zhǎn gōng méi
柳 展 宫 眉，

cuì fú xíng rén shǒu
翠 拂 行 人 首 。

xiàng jiāo yuán tà qīng
向 郊 原 踏 青 ,
zì gē xié shǒu
恣 歌 携 手 。
zuì xūn xūn
醉 醺 醺 、
shàng xún fāng jiǔ
尚 寻 芳 酒 。
wèn mù tóng yáo zhǐ gū cūn
问 牧 童 、 遥 指 孤 村 ,
dào xìng huā shēn chù
道 杏 花 深 处 ,
nà lǐ rén jiā yǒu
那 里 人 家 有 。

Tune: The Way of Brocade

Song Qi

The swallows twittering

Announce spring days are lengthening.

See who into my garden bring

Flowers on flowers like brocade!

Crab apples after rain rouged through like palace maid,

The willow trees with eyebrows spread
Caress with emerald leaves the wayfarer's head.

Out in the green grassland,
We sing our fill, hand in hand.
Drunk with spring fine,
We ask where is a shop of wine.
A cowherd only
Points to a village lonely,
Saying amid apricot flowers
Wine is sold in the bowers.

tà suō xíng
踏莎行

yàn shū
晏 殊

bì hǎi wú bō
碧 海 无 波 ，
yáo tái yǒu lù
瑶 台 有 路 ，
sī liàng biàn hé shuāng fēi qù
思 量 便 合 双 飞 去 。

dāng shí qīng bié yì zhōng rén
当 时 轻 别 意 中 人，
shān cháng shuǐ yuǎn zhī hé chù
山 长 水 远 知 何 处？

qǐ xí níng chén
绮 席 凝 尘，
xiāng guī yǎn wù
香 闺 掩 雾，
hóng jiān xiǎo zì píng shuí fù
红 笺 小 字 凭 谁 附？
gāo lóu mù jìn yù huáng hūn
高 楼 目 尽 欲 黄 昏，
wú tóng yè shàng xiāo xiāo yǔ
梧 桐 叶 上 潇 潇 雨。

Tune: Treading on Grass

Yan Shu

The celestial blue sea is calm and free;
To Heavenly Abode there is a road.
I thought together we'd fly to Paradise on high.
But how could I, light-hearted, with my beloved have pared?
The mountain's high and far, how can I know where you are?

Dust-covered is your velvet seat,
And mist-veiled is your fragrant bower.
How could I send to you my letter sweet?
At dusk I stretch my sight from lofty tower;
On phoenix leaves the rain falls shower by shower.

tà suō xíng
踏莎行

yàn shū
晏殊

xiǎo jìng hóng xī
小径红稀,
fāng jiāo lǜ biàn
芳郊绿遍,
gāo tái shù sè yīn yīn xiàn
高台树色阴阴见。
chūn fēng bù jiě jìn yáng huā
春风不解禁杨花,
méng méng luàn pū xíng rén miàn
蒙蒙乱扑行人面。

cuì yè cáng yīng
翠叶藏莺,
zhū lián gé yàn
珠帘隔燕,

lú xiāng jìng zhú yóu sī zhuǎn
炉 香 静 逐 游 丝 转 。
yì chǎng chóu mèng jiǔ xǐng shí
一 场 愁 梦 酒 醒 时 ,
xié yáng què zhào shēn shēn yuàn
斜 阳 却 照 深 深 院 。

Tune: Treading on Grass

Yan Shu

Along the path red blossoms fade,
On fragrant fields green grass displayed,
By lofty tower trees spread out a dark, dark shade.
The vernal breeze knows not how to keep willow-down
From running riot and making wayfarers frown.

Green leaves hide orioles from sight;
Rearl screens keep out swallows in flight,
Incense from burners wafts like the gossamer light.
When I awake from sorrowful dream and from wine,
In deep deep courtyard peeps the sun on decline.

踏莎行

晏殊

细草愁烟,
幽花怯露,
凭栏总是销魂处。
日高深院静无人,
时时海燕双飞去。

带缓罗衣,
香残蕙炷,
天长不禁迢迢路。
垂杨只解惹春风,
何曾系得行人住?

Tune: Treading on Grass

Yan Shu

The mist-veiled grass looks sad in hue;
Sweet flowers shiver with cold dew.
When she leans on the rails, her heart often bewails.
The courtyard is quiet though advanced is the day;
Now and again a pair of swallows fly away.

Her girdle is too loose her silken dress to tie;
The incense burned up inch by inch will die.
The long long road would vie in length with the wide sky.
The willow branch could bar the vernal breeze from blowing.
Could it ever detain her beloved one from going?

---

tà suō xíng
踏莎行

yàn shū
晏 殊

zǔ xí lí gē
祖 席 离 歌 ,

cháng tíng bié yàn
长 亭 别 宴 ,
xiāng chén yǐ gé yóu huí miàn
香 尘 已 隔 犹 回 面 。
jū rén pǐ mǎ yìng lín sī
居 人 匹 马 映 林 嘶 ,
xíng rén qù zhào yī bō zhuǎn
行 人 去 棹 依 波 转 。

huà gé hún xiāo
画 阁 魂 销 ,
gāo lóu mù duàn
高 楼 目 断 ,
xié yáng zhǐ sòng píng bō yuǎn
斜 阳 只 送 平 波 远 。
wú qióng wú jìn shì lí chóu
无 穷 无 尽 是 离 愁 ,
tiān yá dì jiǎo xún sī biàn
天 涯 地 角 寻 思 遍 。

Tune: Treading on Grass

Yan Shu

The farewell song is sung for you;
We drink our cups and bid adieu,
I look back though fragrant dust keeps you out of view.
My horse going home neighs along the forest wide,

Your sailing boat will go farther with rising tide.

My heart broken in painted bower,
My eyes worn out in lofty tower,
The sun sheds departing rays on the parting one.
Boundless and endless will my sorrow ever run;
On earth or in the sky it will never be done.

qīng píng yuè
清平乐

yàn shū
晏殊

jīn fēng xì xì
金风细细,
yè yè wú tóng zhuì
叶叶梧桐坠。
lǜ jiǔ chū cháng rén yì zuì
绿酒初尝人易醉,
yì zhěn xiǎo chuāng nóng shuì
一枕小窗浓睡。

zǐ wēi zhū jǐn huā cán
紫薇朱槿花残,
xié yáng què zhào lán gān
斜阳却照阑干。

shuāng yàn yù guī shí jié
双 燕 欲 归 时 节,
yín píng zuó yè wēi hán
银 屏 昨 夜 微 寒。

Tune: Pure, Serene Music

Yan Shu

Gently, gently blows golden breeze;
Leaf on leaf falls from phoenix trees.
It's easy to get drunk after tasting green wine;
By small window I soundly nap on pillow mine.

I wake to see red rose and myrtle fade;
The slanting sun peeps at the balustrade.
It's time for swallows' southward flight;
My silver screen was slightly chill last night.

清平乐

晏殊

红笺小字,
说尽平生意。
鸿雁在云鱼在水,
惆怅此情难寄。

斜阳独倚西楼,
遥山恰对帘钩。
人面不知何处,
绿波依旧东流。

Tune: Pure, Serene Music

Yan Shu

On rosy paper a hand fair
Has laid the innermost heart bare.
Nor fish below nor swan above
Would bear this melancholy message of love.

At sunset on west tower alone she stands still;
The curtain hook can't hang up distant hill.
Who know where her beloved is gone?
Green waves still eastward roll on.

dié liàn huā
蝶恋花

yàn shū
晏殊

jiàn jú chóu yān lán qì lù
槛 菊 愁 烟 兰 泣 露 ,
luó mù qīng hán
罗 幕 轻 寒 ,

yàn zǐ shuāng fēi qù
燕子双飞去。
míng yuè bù ān lí hèn kǔ
明月不谙离恨苦,
xié guāng dào xiǎo chuān zhū hù
斜光到晓穿朱户。

zuó yè xī fēng diāo bì shù
昨夜西风凋碧树,
dú shàng gāo lóu
独上高楼,
wàng jìn tiān yá lù
望尽天涯路。
yù jì cǎi jiān jiān chǐ sù
欲寄彩笺兼尺素,
shān cháng shuǐ kuò zhī hé chù
山长水阔知何处?

Tune: Butterflies over Flowers

Yan Shu

Orchids shed tears with doleful asters in mist grey.
How can they stand the cold silk curtains can't allay?
A pair of swallows flies away.
The moon, which knows not parting grief, sheds slanting light
Through crimson windows all the night.

Last night the western breeze
Blew withered leaves off trees.
I mount the tower high
And strain my longing eye.
I'll send a message to my dear,
But endless ranges and streams sever us far and near.

dié liàn huā
蝶恋花

yàn shū
晏 殊

liù qū lán gān wèi bì shù
六 曲 阑 干 偎 碧 树，
yáng liǔ fēng qīng
杨 柳 风 轻，
zhǎn jìn huáng jīn lǚ
展 尽 黄 金 缕。
shuí bǎ diàn zhēng yí yù zhù
谁 把 钿 筝 移 玉 柱？
chuān lián hǎi yàn shuāng fēi qù
穿 帘 海 燕 双 飞 去。

mǎn yǎn yóu sī jiān luò xù
满 眼 游 丝 兼 落 絮，

hóng xìng kāi shí
红 杏 开 时，
yì shà qīng míng yǔ
一 霎 清 明 雨 。
nóng shuì jué lái yīng luàn yǔ
浓 睡 觉 来 莺 乱 语 ，
jīng cán hǎo mèng wú xún chù
惊 残 好 梦 无 寻 处 。

Tune: Butterflies over Flowers

Yan Shu

The winding balustrade caressed by willow trees

Swaying in breeze, displays their golden sprigs with ease.

By whom is played the gilt zither with pegs of jade?

A pair of swallows fly through curtains rolled up high.

The gossamer and willow catkins come in view;

When blow apricot flowers, morning rain falls in showers.

My sound sleep is disturbed by orioles' song anew;

I can no longer find sweet dreams of rosy hue.

浣溪沙

晏殊

一曲新词酒一杯,
去年天气旧亭台。
夕阳西下几时回。

无可奈何花落去,
似曾相识燕归来。
小园香径独徘徊。

Tune: Silk-Washing Stream

Yan Shu

I compose a new song and drink a cup of wine
In the bower of last year when weather is as fine.

When will you come back like the sun on the decline?

Deeply I sigh for the fallen flowers in vain;

Vaguely I seem to know the swallows come again.

Loitering on the garden path, I alone remain.

浣溪沙

晏殊

一向年光有限身,

等闲离别易消魂。

酒筵歌席莫辞频。

满目山河空念远,

落花风雨更伤春。

不如怜取眼前人。

Tune: Silk-Washing Stream

Yan Shu

What can a short-lived man do with the fleeting year
And soul-consuming separations from his dear?
Refuse no banquet when fair singing girls appear!

With hills in sight, I miss the far away in vain.
How can I bear the fallen blooms in wind and rain!
Why not enjoy the fleeting pleasure now again?

山亭柳

晏殊

家住西秦,
赌博艺随身。
花柳上,

斗尖新。
偶学念奴声调,
有时高遏行云。
蜀锦缠头无数,
不负辛勤。

数年来往咸京道,
残杯冷炙漫销魂。
衷肠事,
托何人?
若有知音见采,
不辞遍唱阳春。
一曲当筵落泪,
重掩罗巾。

Tune: Willow by Mountainside Pavilion

Yan Shu

My home was in the west;
I'd vie in talents with the songstress best.
Like blooms or willow trees
I danced new dance with ease.
I learned to sing like pretty palace maid,
Whom floating cloud would stop to hear.
Gifts were showered on me, silk and brocade,
In praise of my skill without peer.

I have traveled for years and suffered a great deal;
It has broken my heart to eat cold meal.
To whom can I confide
My grief and wounded pride?
If there's a connoisseur to come along,
I won't refuse to sing for him my best song.
One song sung at the feast, how could my tears not rain?
With silken handherchief I'd hide my face again.

玉楼春

春恨

晏殊

绿杨芳草长亭路,
年少抛人容易去。
楼头残梦五更钟,
花底离愁三月雨。

无情不似多情苦,
一寸还成千万缕。
天涯地角有穷时,
只有相思无尽处。

Tune: Spring in Jade Pavilion
Spring Grief

Yan Shu

Farewell pavilion green with grass and willow trees!
How could my gallant young lord have left me with ease!
I'm woke by midnight bell from dim dream in my bower;
Parting grief won't part with flowers falling in shower.

My beloved feels no sorrow my loving heart sheds;
Each string as woven with thousands of painful threads.
However far and wide the sky and earth may be,
They can't measure the lovesickness o'erwhelming me.

huàn xī shā
浣溪沙

yàn shū
晏 殊

xiǎo gé chóng lián yǒu yàn guò
小 阁 重 帘 有 燕 过 ,

晚花红片落庭莎，
曲阑干影入凉波。

一霎好风生翠幕，
几回疏雨滴圆荷？
酒醒人散得愁多。

Tune: Silk-Washing Stream

Yan Shu

By double-curtained bower I see swallows pass;
Red petals of late flowers fall on courtyard grass,
The winding rails' shadow mingles with ripples cold.

A sudden gale blows and ruffles emerald screen.
How many times has rain dripped on lotus leaves green?
Awake from wine, the grief to see guests gone makes me old.

离亭燕

张昇

一带江山如画,
风物向秋潇洒。
水浸碧天何处断?
霁色冷光相射。
蓼屿荻花洲,
掩映竹篱茅舍。

云际客帆高挂,
烟外酒旗低亚。
多少六朝兴废事,
尽入渔樵闲话。
怅望倚层楼,
寒日无言西下。

Tune: Swallows Leaving Pavilion

Zhang Bian

So picturesque the land by riverside,
In autumn tints the scenery is purified.
Without a break green waves merge into azure sky,
The sunbeams after rain take chilly dye.
Bamboo fence dimly seen amid the reeds
And thatch-roofed cottages overgrown with weeds.

Among white clouds are lost white sails,
And where smoke coils up slow,
There wineshop streamers hang low.
How many of the fisherman's and woodman's tales
Are told about the Six Dynasties' fall and rise!
Saddened, I lean upon the tower's rails,
Mutely the sun turns cold and sinks in western skies.

千秋岁

张先

数声鹈鴂,
又报芳菲歇。
惜春更把残红折。
雨轻风色暴,
梅子青时节。
永丰柳,
无人尽日飞花雪。

莫把幺弦拨,
怨极弦能说。
天不老,
情难绝。
心似双丝网,
中有千千结。
夜过也,
东南未白凝残月。

Tune: A Thousand Autumns

Zhang Xian

The cuckoo showers
Tears of adieu on fallen flowers.
Lovers of spring would pluck a sprig of fading red.
Light drizzle and strong breeze
Have greened mume trees.
All day long no one sees the willow-down
Like snow or flowers dead waft up and down.

Don't pluck the lonely string,
Or of grief it will sing.
The sky never grows old;
Love won't turn cold.
Like a silken net is my heart;
I can't untie its thousand knots nor set them apart.
The night will pass away;
The waning moon is frozen before the break of day.

诉衷情

张先

花前月下暂相逢,
苦恨阻从容。
何况酒醒梦断,
花谢月朦胧?

花不尽,
月无穷,
两心同。
此时愿作,
杨柳千丝,
绊惹春风。

Tune: Telling of Innermost Feeling

Zhang Xian

Before flowers, beneath the moon, shortly we met
Only to part with bitter regret.
What's more, I wake from wine and dreams
To find fallen flowers and dim moonbeams.

Flowers will bloom again;
The moon will wax and wane.
Would our hearts be the same?
I'd turn the flame
Of my heart, string on string,
Into willow twigs to retain the breeze of spring.

一丛花

张先

伤高怀远几时穷?
无物似情浓。
离愁正引千丝乱,
更东陌、
飞絮蒙蒙。
嘶骑渐遥,
征尘不断,
何处认郎踪?

双鸳池沼水溶溶,
南北小桡通。
梯横画阁黄昏后,
又还是、
斜月帘栊。
沉恨细思,

bù rú táo xìng,
不 如 桃 杏，
yóu jiě jià dōng fēng。
犹 解 嫁 东 风。

Tune: Song of Flower Shrub

Zhang Xian

When will the sorrow end to watch my parting friend
From a tower above? Nothing's so deep as love.
My sorrow interweaves a thousand twigs of leaves;
The pathway east of the town
Is shrouded in wafting willow-down.
His neighing steed is far away.
A cloud of dust still darkening the day.
Where is the place to find his trace?

A pair of lovebirds seem to melt in water clean:
Little leaflike boats go north and south, to and fro.
After dusk in twilight
I dare not mount the painted bower on the height.
What will again be seen

But the waning moon shining on window screen?
How deeply I envy peach and apricot trees
Newly wed to and oft caressed by vernal breeze!

菩萨蛮 (pú sà mán)

张先 (zhāng xiān)

忆郎还上层楼曲,
楼前芳草年年绿。
绿似去时袍,
回头风袖飘。

郎袍应已旧,
颜色非长久。
惟恐镜中春,
不如花草新。

Tune: Buddhist Dancers

Zhang Xian

Missing my lord, I lean on railings of the tower;
From year to year sweet grass turns green before my bower.
Green as the gown he wore on taking leave.
Turning his head, the wind wafted his sleeve.

His gown must be outworn and old.
How can its green color long hold?
I fear my mirrored spring, alas!
Cannot renew as bloom and grass.

tiān xiān zǐ
天 仙 子

zhāng xiān
张 先

shuǐ diào　　shù shēng chí jiǔ tīng
《水 调》数 声 持 酒 听，

wǔ zuì xǐng lái chóu wèi xǐng
午 醉 醒 来 愁 未 醒。
sòng chūn chūn qù jǐ shí huí
送 春 春 去 几 时 回?
lín wǎn jìng
临 晚 镜,
shāng liú jǐng
伤 流 景,
wǎng shì hòu qī kōng jì xǐng
往 事 后 期 空 记 省。

shā shàng bìng qín chí shàng míng
沙 上 并 禽 池 上 暝,
yún pò yuè lái huā nòng yǐng
云 破 月 来 花 弄 影。
chóng chóng lián mù mì zhē dēng
重 重 帘 幕 密 遮 灯。
fēng bú dìng
风 不 定,
rén chū jìng
人 初 静,
míng rì luò hóng yīng mǎn jìng
明 日 落 红 应 满 径。

Tune: Song of the Immortal

Zhang Xian

Wine cup in hand, I listen to "Water Melody",
Awake from wine at noon but not from melancholy.

When will spring come back now it is going away?
In the mirror, alas!
I see happy time pass.
In vain may I recall the old days gone for aye.

Night falls on poolside sand where pairs of lovebirds stay;
The moon breaks through the clouds; with shadows flowers play.
Lamplight is veiled by screen on screen;
The fickle wind still blows,
The night so silent grows.
Tomorrow fallen blooms on the way will be seen.